stories of love

Forever and a Day

bright sky press
340 South Second Street, Albany, Texas 76430
and
New York, New York

Library of Congress Cataloging-in-Publication Data

Sander, Norbert W.
    Forever and a day : stories of love / Norbert W. Sander.
        p. cm.
    ISBN 1-931721-02-5 (alk. paper)
    1. Love stories. American. I. Title.
    PS3569.A486 F67 2002
    813'.54—dc21

                                                        2002016335

            9 8 7 6 5 4 3 2 1

Book design by Kathryn W. Plosica / Two Rivers Design

PRINTED IN CHINA

stories of love

Forever and a Day

Norbert W. Sander, M.D.

I dedicate this to Bridget, to my beloved children,
my mother, my father, to my sister and my brother,
to all of my loyal family, to my dear and cherished friends
and to all those who have helped and supported me
in whatever way, large or small.

INTRODUCTION

e. cummings once said that "love is the mystery of mysteries." And so it remains, though something tangible can be said of it: that it differs between people and that one's love varies in kind and intensity as between husband and wife, lover and loved, parent and child, between two friends, even between two enemies. There is no finite store of love in each of us. It is bottomless and need never run out, though often the show of it can be so craftfully disguised and even paralyzed. Love is in the little contacts with each other, the repository of familiar warmth and trust and attraction. It is in the knowing as in how a certain woman softly pulls up her sheer black stockings or how much brown sugar your younger brother, rumpled in his pajamas at the kitchen table, used to so carefully spread over his hot oatmeal on winter mornings. Love seems rarely to last on the grand scale, a drama difficult to constantly sustain before it dissipates and drifts into curious memory. Though, too, a man and a woman are their memories and their imagination very much as well.

This collection is an attempt at the shades of love, its subtleties, heartbreak and limitations, but also an effort to reach for its potential. The pursuit of love is what is left most for us to accomplish in life, its reward the glory of glories, but if we are to fall short it is the journey that counts most. There is no shame in the effort and despite all, there is in the very end the possibility of redemption and always the knowledge that we will surely live to find real love another day.

LOVING YOU

There are some who have married for money, some for fame, others for desire, and still others out of loneliness. I have married mainly for liking the woman who is my wife, not always, of course, but nearly always.

I like her innocence, even though at times it's lost in anger. I like her memory, which often turns against me if I am sloppy in recall. And I like the time she has for others, how it's not measured or withheld. I like her naturalness and lack of pretense, and the way she can so easily be offended yet still find it hard to carry a grudge. I like that she worries about me and my health and I think someday I may truly need her help. I like her curiosity and her love of small indulgences that allow for a glass of good wine and even a small cigar. I like her deep auburn hair and bright, unchanging smile, and how we nestle warmly in our generous, soft bed and how the early-morning light runs silently across her porcelain-white face. And, too, I like the excitement in her voice as she calls loudly to our young daughters announcing that I am home.

I like and love her. We are not perfect together nor were we meant to be. We are apart in age yet there is a respect for our differences. With her I feel a true hope for the future. I trust in her basic goodness, a goodness I have learned from as she, in whatever unique way, I hope, has learned from me. We will keep on loving each other yet, if we do not, we will have only our ungrateful selves to blame. But we will keep on loving each other. I am sure of that.

LE PRINTEMPS
Marc Chagall

PURITY

I first saw her through a small, distant window as she lay quietly asleep. Only her petite, finely shaped head with its surprisingly rosy cheeks stuck out from under two firmly wrapped covers. She faced the ceiling and, despite the bright lights above, her tiny eyelids remained peacefully drawn.

She had come on what her purposeful, deep breathing said was a long journey. She was tired but obviously content, replenishing her resources spent in the struggle she had just left behind. An aura of calm triumph had settled over her small, unmoving mouth. One voyage was completed. She would soon be ready for the next.

As I watched my newborn daughter so intently from behind the glass in the midnight hours of the hospital nursery, I resisted the impulse to look beyond that moment. The beauty of watching her minuscule body motionless in time, unburdened of all responsibility, bereft of all expectation, unfettered from all emotion of love, of wrath, of jealousy, of joy or dislike, the pleasure of that still moment was all I wished to savor and all I wished to somehow convey to her: that I and her mother, now lying exhausted in the room next door, would pledge to be at her side always, knowing nothing more about her—nothing more than that beautiful sight of her lying there so quietly, confidently, so serenely poised to begin her life.

THE THREE AGES OF WOMAN

Gustav Klimt

WALTZING AT THE RITZ

They say for every boy and girl
There is just one love in this whole world
and I've found mine.

SONNY JAMES

would in general like to be able to dance better. The waltz that is. It is probably true of most men, especially my age. There is a certain romance to it that is hard to get at otherwise. Actually there was a time when I could waltz and pretty respectably.

Mrs. McNamara's School of Ballroom Dancing is where we went on Friday nights when I was twelve. For one dollar we boys got to dress up with a wide garish tie, usually our father's, and learn all the dances in Mrs. McNamara's basement. We also got an incredible chance to meet the girls we went to school with, actually touch them, hold them, their most exquisite hands and shoulders and in some cases exposed backs, dressed freshly in perfumed pastels of light blue or pink.

I often danced with Patricia Kelly who later became the great love of my early teens. She said, respectfully as girls would then, that I was a good dancer even as I stepped clumsily and repeatedly on the soft, demure toes of her pink pumps. Still the nights there gave us confidence, an introduction to style, and our first look at romance. I have since lost the rhythm but there are quiet moments when I can again feel my hand around Patricia's waist, my perspiring palm holding hers as we spin and turn slowly, elegantly, around and around the linoleum of Mrs. McNamara's ballroom, lost in the strains of her gramophone, lost in the easy, soft steps of a Viennese waltz.

BLUE DANCERS
Edgar Degas

FIRST KISS

Love at the lips was touch
As sweet as I could bear;
And once that seemed too much;
I lived on air.

ROBERT FROST

A first kiss can be prolonged, consciously drawn out, or short and tender. It can be tentative and miss the mark or confident under a blazing sun, on a beach or in a driving rain or leaning impulsively across a checkered tablecloth in a quiet restaurant just after dessert and coffee or even struck in the shadows of a movie theater near the end of a film like *Breakfast at Tiffany's*. It can be sudden and intense, driven by desire and too much lusty red wine or it can be exchanged on soft green grass even before the picnic basket is ever opened. A first kiss can be won at spin the bottle, the pleasure of touching such young, eager lips so exhilarating or it can be even more thoughtful and profound such as when you and she stopped to talk beside the old stone wall, the brightness of that late-fall afternoon blanching even more across the thinning white hair on both your heads.

A first kiss is both a beginning and an end. You cannot take it back or give it away again. It may be trivialized and easily forgotten or that one fleeting, anxious, sublime moment may be held in memory for a lifetime, coloring the perception of all the other kisses you may ever give or so expectantly receive from the elusive yet ever-constant lips of your love.

TRIPTYCH OF THE DAY

Gaetano Previati

THE WILD
BLUE YONDER

Oh, I have slipped the surly bonds of earth,
And danced the skies on laughter-silvered wings.

JOHN GILLESPIE MAGEE, JR.

Flying with my father is one of the best memories I have of my parents together. He loved seaplanes and it was often late in the day when we taxied out onto the water, the early-winter sun beaming optimistically through the high cloud formations. Tucked in securely behind them, I'd watch with wonderment the foamy seawater scattering from the plane's pontoons as we lifted gloriously from Long Island Sound and headed north along the Connecticut coast. Once we were airborne my father would excitedly point out the landmarks then bank and loop and dive and climb and land with much ceremony on the open sea, instructing my mother and me to hold our breath again as the plane reskimmed the water surface, struggling to break free and rise up into the unpopulated sky.

Life, however, was less certain with my father down on earth. A reckless man, he bent to his own impulses, often chasing good times, drink, and flight, both here and on foreign shores. But when he was with us he gave me much—the fruits of his prolific reading, the sharp, incisive opinions of a strangely honorable man, and of course an expert's view of aviation. He spoke of Lindbergh, Earhart, Corrigan, the dynamics of a perfect wing as he held his balsa-wood models up to the light, and his predictions that someday planes would fly without propellers and would incredibly exceed the speed of sound.

Flight was our release, too, and on those late autumn afternoons in the open sky with the noise of the plane's engine deafening to my young ears, I felt close to my parents, high above life's troubles. It made me fearless and liberated and eager to join them in what could only seem like a spectacular adventure.

FIELD UNDER THUNDERCLOUDS
Vincent van Gogh

MAKING LOVE IN A
FOREIGN LANGUAGE

This is what youth must figure out:
Girls, love, and living.
The having, the not having,
The spending and the giving.
And the melancholy time of not knowing.

E.B. WHITE

first experienced this in a phone booth. As a teenager, even on bone-cold winter nights, you still made important calls outside the house. For me, down at the local Texaco station, Eddie's. I would go there to call this new girlfriend of mine.

Pamela was fourteen, beautiful, exquisite, blond, with perfect hair and full young lips. She was a model and wore leopard-skin hats. We usually saw her picture in magazines.

My friend Vincent, for unclear reasons, rejected her overtures, and Pamela turned her interest to me. After two dates, a movie, and a ride to get ice cream in my father's Pontiac, I found myself one night in the booth at Eddie's. We were chatting when Pamela's voice grew very quiet, even a bit intimate.

"You know," she said.

"Yes?" I replied. And then, in the most fetching voice, Pamela murmured into the phone, "Je t'aime."

I was stumped, stone quiet.

"You know what I just said?"

"Of course I do," I answered awkwardly.

I have since learned French—even once, several years ago, received a compliment from a local in Provence. But I am still reluctant to use it when it comes to love. About the missed chance with Pamela, I'd like to have it over again. This time I'd tell her that I'd be right over so she could slowly, in person, repeat what she'd just said, so that I could understand it all, the foreign language that is, much better.

JEANNE HEBUTERNE
Amadeo Modigliani

FRIDAY NIGHTS

The time you won your town the race
We chaired you through the market place;
Man and boy stood cheering by,
And home we brought you shoulder-high.

A.E. HOUSMAN

My grandfather lived alone across the courtyard in our apartment house. He loved sports. Television was new and he and I would watch for hours on end together. He didn't say much during the games, so we watched quietly.

We liked the fights, especially the Cavalcade of Sports on Friday nights, one of which had BoBo Olsen facing the great Sugar Ray Robinson for the middleweight crown. Olsen, prematurely balding, had all he could handle in Robinson, an extraordinary boxer who could knock out an opponent with either hand and was dangerous even in retreat. As the bout progressed, Olsen just didn't look himself, his legs flat and listless. The television commentator then added that his wife had just left him, a shocking thing to reveal on television in those days. Olsen looked so lonely out there in the ring. I began to feel sorry for him. Just moments later Robinson connected with one of his specialty punches and Olsen went down. He struggled to get up but it was all over. My grandfather looked sadly over at me. I nodded back.

We shared many football games as well and jumped up and down like kids when Notre Dame broke Oklahoma's record-winning streak. Our last game was actually in Philadelphia. He took me there to see Army play Navy. My grandfather was sick then, dying of cancer, though he never told me. That day Navy's star halfback dazzled the record crowd and sent his team to the Cotton Bowl. Afterward my grandfather and I walked along the Army sidelines and mixed with the players.

On the plane back my grandfather began to vomit and grow weak. The steward had to steady him, and my uncles met us at the airport. He died peacefully two weeks later. I felt then the same irrevocable loss that Olsen must have felt when he went down and couldn't get up. For me those championship years with my grandfather, so private and engrossing, so joyful and at times so sad, were over.

DEMPSEY AND FIRPO
George Wesley Bellows

POTS AND KETTLES

Through you I knew Woman and did not fear her spell.

PATRICK KAVANAGH

In 1945, one early evening when it was pitch-dark, my mother said we could go out on the street in front of out apartment house and make noise. She handed me a dented pot and a metal ladle and said I should bang it as loudly as I could. That day World War II had just ended.

The pot, rippled and loose at the handle, was the one my mother cooked hot pudding in for our desserts. It was usually chocolate and occasionally butterscotch, a thick, delicious, creamy liquid that we poured slowly into clear glass cups, being ever so careful to distribute this delectable treat evenly. When the pouring was done, a thin layer of cooling warm pudding remained at the bottom, and when it was your turn, our mother supplied a soup spoon and you got your chance, before dinner, to lick the pot.

Though our apartment was postage-stamp-sized, my mental image of my mother is of her in front of the stove presiding over our meals, our snacks, our friends, and the steady flow of visitors who would come unannounced in search of an egg, some bread, a cup of milk, medicines, advice, jokes, stories and at times comfort from the hardships of daily life. Our kitchen table was our day's beginning, our source of warm soup at lunch, our shared supper at night. It was also a café where much beer and wine were drunk and cigarettes smoked amid discussion that as children we listened to quietly, marveling at the animated stories and exotic tales of bravery, daring, travel, intimacy, and at times, treachery and cowardice.

I have not been disappointed as an adult with the preparation I received for life from my mother's kitchen, the center of our home. Her message lives on: to grab the pot and bang it as loudly as you can, join in the celebration of life, cherish your family table and give of it more than you expect to receive, and be sure in pouring the pudding that each cup is equitably filled, and if at the end there is some left over and it is your turn, roll up your sleeves, take up your ladle and enjoy the warm, sweet pleasure of licking the pot.

STILL LIFE WITH POMEGRANATES

Henri Matisse

MY SISTER

And you ate an apple, and I ate a pear,
From a dozen of each we had bought somewhere;
And the sky went wan, and the wind came cold,
And the sun rose dripping, a bucketful of gold.

EDNA ST. VINCENT MILLAY

On my block we generally made it a point to avoid our sisters. Even if you ever entertained a crumb of interest in including your sister in anything, even in toasting marshmallows at a picnic, you would never risk the mockery of that scruffy band of boys you spent every waking hour of every day with.

So I didn't really know my sister. When our younger brother died, Carroll and I were in our early forties. She said to me when we first embraced, "You and I are the only ones left." But I wasn't thinking about us. I was thinking more about him. He was the one missing. The rest of us, as far as I was concerned, were still here.

When my sister graduated from nursing school and began to work professionally, my feelings began to change toward her, not only because I had changed but because she had as well. She had developed opinions, demanded my respect, challenged me, and yet, I must admit, I often acted as if I was still in the neighborhood playing marbles on a worn dirt patch, expecting Carroll to be looking over my shoulder, watching but saying nothing.

Today we don't always believe in exactly the same things, but we are able to listen to each other with great interest, usually without interrupting. When I am about to take a long trip, usually an adventure, she will often call at the last minute to say good-bye. As I am getting off and she has just said how much she cares for me, my voice sometimes cracks and I get emotional. Even concealed a bit on the other side of the phone, watery eyes and stuffy nose, I am still very happy to feel that way, to feel so gratefully my dear sister's love.

ARTIST'S STUDIO IN VENICE
Raoul Dufy

REMEMBERING VIETNAM

And in that time
When men decide and feel safe
To call the war insane
Take one moment to embrace
Those gentle heroes you left behind.

MAJOR
MICHAEL DAVIS O'DONNELL

My brother died well after the Vietnam War was over. When I asked if his name could be inscribed on the memorial in Washington, they said it was not possible. To get there, someone else had to kill you.

How he got himself into the thick of the war there as a young Marine is still a painful memory for my family and me. I was in medical school when my brother was sending home dirt-stained letters, fighting hand to hand, at times taking the life from teenagers his own age. He also witnessed his comrades hanging upside down from trees, disemboweled by the enemy, and heard primal cries for help from captured Marines, unable to be saved, while they were tortured and slowly put to death. When he was shot after nearly two years of much-decorated combat, then saved with a colostomy bag in place, he considered it a deliverance.

My brother's years after the war were turbulent. He found little success and there were long periods in Veterans Administration hospitals, sometimes in stress units. When he ended his life, it was the most desperately painful moment I could ever expect to experience in a lifetime. Now, ten years later, I think about him often—his pride, his innocence, his courage, and his basic honesty—and wish if only somehow he could be given another chance to come back and try life all over again.

HORIZONS
Jeff Dodge

THE POLLYWOG POND

But we in it shall be remembered
We few, we happy few, we band of brothers

WILLIAM SHAKESPEARE

s it possible to love a place as much as one does a person? Paris, Connemara, Key West, or a bubbling brook in upstate New York can make you cherish them with the same kind of unambivalent passion. And each place holds its memories: the warmth of familiarity, the boisterous ecstatic laughter you once roared in its streets, the sweet wet smell of grass at a country house in early summer, year after year, the slow but certain change of seasons, the constancy of every new cycle of flower and trees, the tap-dancing on your farmhouse roof as frantic, fat squirrels make ready for winter.

I have loved a particular place in that way. Behind my apartment house and through a ragged woods with well-worn rooted paths, I came when I was young to a muddy spring no more than 12 yards across. I went there in all seasons and at all times of day: in spring, when deep, verdant weeds encircled its littered shore; in summer, when thick brown frogs had grown noisily from secretive tadpoles, when stifling heat would drive us out in torn underwear into its muddy water and down to its slimy bottom cushioned with decades of collecting leaves. My friends and I came to this pond on damp, still nights to gather together and to share quietly in the dark the embarrassed secrets of our households. In the chill we came, usually alone, early in the morning when no one else was about, to be silent and feel the gathering breeze behind the withering grass. We built up a stone border to make the pond deeper and dug cool huts with sagging roofs into its high dirt banks. We broke rich milkweeds and put the creamy elixir on each other's skin, swearing to return in ten or twenty or thirty years to this place to be together again.

WATERLILIES
Claude Monet

LE CAFÉ HOT

People ask me: Why do you write about food and eating and drinking?
Why don't you write about the struggle for power and security, and about love,
The way others do? The easiest answer is to say that, like most other humans,
I am hungry.

BOB SHACOCHIS

I have a dream. This is my own idea. It's been developing, slowly. It's a dream about owning a restaurant, actually a diner, a drive-in diner, well known but not too well known, where people will come from all over in late-model unusual cars, preferably convertibles, to eat at my Café Hot. There will be more to it than just food. I want everyone to have a good time, too, with me, with the music, even a bit with the family—the missus, who sings very good, and the little ones, who I will make sure will not always be there.

Regarding the menu: Pepper is the unkept secret in my food—red, black or white. I also mince yellow, orange, and green bell peppers, and add, of course, garlic and curry and rosemary and anise seed. They have the character, the bite. I like peanut butter and put it on our fried potatoes, and Tabasco which always goes on the rice, and fennel which I sprinkle on the steaks. Here in Le Café Hot, I'm afraid the salads are secondary, but the bread is prime, the cheese is pungent and the desserts très riche. My favorites are gently sautéed fruits with just enough Drambuie and fresh cream.

The music will be upbeat with plenty of fiddles, but there will be quiet time too. In addition, if you like, you will get a chance to get up and say something yourself, such as a poem or sing an old standard in which we can all join along. My good friends, of course, will be there on a steady basis and the reception will be warm. I am sure we will all get to know one another.

Last week on Route 9, I passed the almost perfect place. The diner was abandoned, but I could see the booths looked pretty good and the counter and stools were just what I had in mind. The parking lot was my only worry. It seemed a bit too small for the size of the cars and for the number of people I figure, when they hear about Le Café Hot, will want to be coming.

LUNCHEON OF THE BOATING PARTY
Pierre-Auguste Renoir

PASSION FRUIT

I drank my first bottle of red Bordeaux in a French bistro with bright red leather banquettes on Forty-third street in New York City. It was Saint Emilion. I was young and in love. We were on our way to see Richard Burton play Hamlet on Broadway. Everything was perfect. The food, the excitement, the expectations but especially the wine. The wine was just splendid.

For love, of course, not just any wine will do. You want the wine with personality, with character, and with a future. Decent red wine carefully chosen can fill the bill. To begin, pick a wine that captures the moment, the food, and the season. Heavier wines do better in winter and in the rain, the Bordeaux, the cabernets. Lighter, finer wines, the Burgundies, and the pinot noires are for anytime, but nicer in the spring and fall. For the summer why not a chilled Beaujolais?

In the company of your love, sequestered at a quiet table, choose your wine with care. Cost is not the first issue. Timing is. You want the wine that is ready, that gives a fine color up to the light, that makes a good first impression.

Let the wine follow you into the meal, let it linger in your fingertips as you look up into the eyes of your amour across the table, let it meander lazily into dessert. You may stop there, or taste a sherry or a port to finish, though in every sense you've just begun. The full beauty of the evening is just before you.

STRANGER IN PARADISE
Christian Pierre

TIMING

Oh, never a doubt but, somewhere I shall wake,
And give what's left of love again, and make new friends, now strangers....

RUPERT BROOKE

When they stepped into the taxi and began heading uptown, both of them began to have doubts at the same time. Walter had never met Judy before. Judy had only a muffled conversation to go on, but Walter's voice just didn't seem right. When they agreed for their first date to meet under the clock at Grand Central Station, he said he had black hair and would be wearing a bright red tie. But he clearly had light brown hair and no tie at all.

"I'm glad I got here early," Judy said as they settled in,

"Me too," Walter said.

"We'll be ahead of the rush at the restaurant."

"Restaurant?" Judy said, turning quickly to him. "I thought we were going to a movie."

Walter hesitated nervously.

"I'm sorry. Did I say a movie? I meant we were going to a restaurant. You'll like it — Northern Italian."

Judy raised her eyebrows and looked out the taxi window. Neither of them spoke as the cabbie whistled along north up Park Avenue. Walter could tell in ten seconds on a blind date when it wasn't going to work. No real attraction. He wished he could open the door and jump out, right then and there. Judy was also becoming more concerned. What type of person would go so far as to disguise himself or to be so devious about his appearance? She glanced over at Walter, checking for a toupee. The brown hair was real.

"You don't seem like the person I spoke with on the phone," Judy said.

"You know, that's what I'm thinking about you," Walter answered. "I mean you told me you were tall and thin."

"I don't remember mentioning anything about my size except for the blond hair."

"I thought you said black," Walter answered.

"There is some mistake here," Judy said, and suddenly asked the taxi to pull over.

"I'm getting out. Maybe another time, Walter."

"Sure, that will be fine," he answered, both relieved and perplexed.

Judy got out and hailed a cab to take her to the station to find the train back to Mount Vernon. Walter stayed on and directed the driver back to his apartment on east Twenty-third Street. As his taxi was going south on Park Avenue, another cab was heading north, and they passed each other unnoticed at Fifty-seventh Street. Judith, a tall, thin black-haired woman was getting to know Wally, a slightly plump dark-haired man with a loud tie with whom she was going out for the first time. They had just met, as planned, under the clock at Grand Central Station and seemed already to be enjoying themselves, each apologizing profusely for, as usual, not being on time. Judith thought Wally was cute, and he was telling himself that he always knew in less than a minute whether he was going to like a woman. Boy, was he excited.

CITYSCAPE
John Marin

MONSIEUR, MADAME AND THE DOG

Henri de Toulouse-Lautrec

DRESSING UP

I can't be talkin' of love, dear,
I can't be talkin' of love
If there be one thing I can't talk of
That one thing do be love.

ESTHER MATHEWS

Gilbert had been looking forward to this night. It's not often you get a chance to dance at the Rainbow Room. He tried to imagine the music they might play. Helen was excited, too, but she wasn't showing it. Sitting through a litany of retirement speeches for her brother-in-law, John, would probably take the luster from the night. Besides, she did not like John's wife and she had no intention of sitting next to her. She also didn't have a dress that was up to Rainbow Room standards.

"We're running late, Helen."

"Don't rush me, Gilbert, I'm going as fast as I can."

Helen was looking for her stockings. She had forgotten to buy new ones and was looking through her drawer for something to match her standard black dress. Gilbert was always ready on time. He took good care of himself as he would say, "first and foremost," laying out his socks and underwear carefully then polishing his shoes before showering to keep his hands clean. Once dressed, he paced the house waiting for Helen often following her from room to room.

"You can be nerve-racking, Gilbert. Why don't you walk the dog?"

"He went out this afternoon."

"I know. I walked him myself. Take him again, Gilbert, while I get ready."

"I am ready, that's the difference, Helen."

"Men get away with murder. They wear the same thing every time."

"Sounds like someone I know."

"What does that mean, Gilbert?"

"You should have dressed up more, at least this time, " he said.

"Give me the money and I will."

"You didn't ask."

"It's because I already know the answer," she said.

"Fine, don't ask."

"Fine, don't expect anymore," she answered.

Helen was pulling her dress over her head. Gilbert was watching in the doorway from behind her.

"Gilbert," she shouted.

"I'm right here," he answered.

"Oh, can you zip me up?"

He walked over and slowly zipped up her dress, pausing when he finished to kiss her gently on the nape of her neck. She began to pull away, annoyed, then hesitated.

"Do that again," she said.

He leaned over and gently kissed her a second time.

"That's much better," she said.

"Ready?"

"Ready," Helen answered.

WEST WITH THE DAWN

All legendary obstacles lay between
us, the long imaginary plain,
The monstrous ruck of mountains

JOHN MONTAGUE

Clare was a woman who preferred the company of men. Most at home up to her knees in a trout stream than kneeling in a circle at a baby shower, she was a certain kind of woman, a man's woman so to speak. Relishing the outdoors, hiking anywhere without complaint, and drinking with the best, she was very good company and a patient listener. For me it would have been an ideal friendship except that I wanted more, much more.

You see Clare was a beautiful woman. How could I ignore that fact? It was something that colored all my thinking. When she rode, you would have seen what I mean: that free flowing chestnut hair, big deep brown eyes and thin hips, casually holding in that foolish horse. Confidence and ease, a monied ease, only more natural, without the calculated training.

There was another side to Clare. As accomplished as she was with a shot-gun or at the controls of a Piper Cub, or in the satin pleasures of the night, Claire was coldly indifferent to children—not only her own child, but to all others. With time I sensed a growing lack of tolerance for the juvenile in me also, my occasional silliness, my irreverence. As soft as those caresses felt on the nape of my neck or as savory her jocular, dry champagne—the touch, the taste, the pleasure of it all began to grow stale and I knew it was time to move on.

THE BLUE RIDER

Wassily Kandinsky

DANCING WITH MEN

This is what age must learn about...
The going, yet not going
The loving and leaving
And the unbearable knowing and knowing.

E.B. WHITE

A woman who was eighty said it was okay if I rolled down her stockings. I had to strap a wire on her legs to do an electrocardiogram. She needed help.

"It's been a long time since anyone did that to me," she said.

"Oh," I answered.

"It feels pretty good," she offered.

"Well, I'm moving things along," I said, a bit embarrassed.

"You know, doctor, I miss my husband so. I think of him every day."

"Are you lonely?"

"I am, for these past ten years, more than you know."

"Why don't you join a club, plan trips?"

"I don't like trips," she said, "I like to dance."

"Then go to dances."

"I do. I go all the time."

"That's good," I said.

"I know," she answered, "but when I dance, I have a rule."

"What's that?"

"I dance, but only with men."

Her left eye winked the most perfect wink. I was envious. I have always wanted to control that one part of my face with such a knowing gesture. For me it only ends up in distorted lines and furrows, especially right in the middle of my forehead. I looked back at her, but by now the wink was gone and she was hurrying to pull up her stockings. She said she was late and had someplace to go.

DANCE IN THE COUNTRY
Pierre-Auguste Renoir

WITH A BROOM IN MY HAND

He questioned softly why I failed?
"For beauty," I replied.
"And I for truth, the two are one;
We brethren are," he said.

EMILY DICKINSON

On August 20, 1829, Mr. E. Linch, a Shaker, left his community to look for strawberries and did not return. Tired of his celibate life, he was off merrily to join in the world of the flesh. Elder Fredric Evans, a contemporary, might have regretted the other man's defection but did not mourn: "The joys of a celibate life are far greater that I can make you know. They are indescribable." It is unlikely Brother E. Linch held the same ardor, but thousands of other Shakers did.

For over one hundred years, Shakerism thrived in communities from New England to Kentucky, espousing the strict separation of the sexes, brotherly love, and emotional catharsis through ecstatic group dancing. The Shakers found closeness to the deity here on earth in the form of creation: the most perfect architecture of their buildings and exquisite design of their home furnishings. Despite their numerous accomplishments, however, by the mid-twentieth century, they had successfully unreproduced themselves into oblivion.

What lasts now of the Shakers is more than their furniture. They have managed to pass on an interpretation of love clearly out of sync with today's language. The "Big I," Sister Elizabeth Lovegrove wrote in 1830, must be tempered in favor of "the common sound." Love was a measure of perfection. Love, too, was a freedom from unwanted yokes. It was the company of others. It could be found in symmetry — symmetry of mind, body, and surroundings. Though the Shakers are now essentially extinct, a curious wind still blows through their empty settlements and down their finely polished hallways, perplexing yet the anxious sleep of modern times.

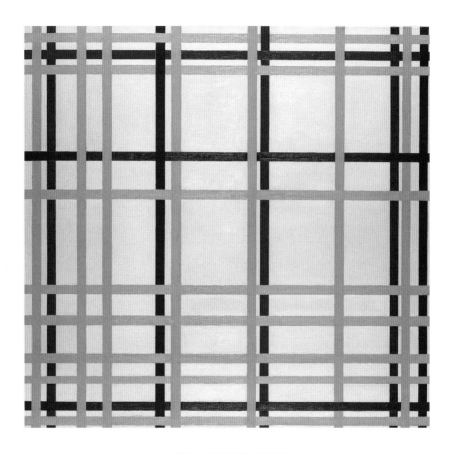

NEW YORK CITY
Piet Mondrian

GIFTS

Light breaks where no sun shines;
Where no sea runs, the waters of the heart
Push in their tides;

DYLAN THOMAS

O n certain uninteresting Saturdays when life in our town had turned a bit dull, my father would take my brother down to Philadelphia, to get a haircut. It was an unusual gesture, especially then, since we lived in New York. The junket in my father's mind necessitated a plane trip which began at LaGuardia Airport in Queens and was punctuated by the obligatory call from a barbershop on Court Street to my mother describing in excited detail the deft strokes being then delivered to my brother's young scalp. Her response was far less enthusiastic, my father having last been seen quietly leaving our apartment that morning with a carefully prepared grocery list in his back pocket.

For a grown man, my father was self-centered, irresponsible, and at times adolescent. There was, however, a certain style in his extremes, an ability to both disappoint and endear at the same time. He could make the preposterous seem possible, could paint a picture much larger than anyone about him and knew when and when not to offer the beau geste, even when he himself doubted his ability to back up his words.

He was a man of high adventure. Who else would have boarded a tramp steamer for Shanghai just after his sixteenth birthday, or spent his eighteenth in Australia, or his nineteenth in Mexico, or his twentieth in Toronto, attempting to fly in the Battle of Britain well before Pearl Harbor? His life as a father did little to curb his energies. He expected, he said, to be a long time dead and wished not for longevity but for "fifty good years." His tombstone records that he received a bonus of no more than several brief months.

But I remember him most at Christmas when his penchant for heavy drinking could often spin out of control. Despite this he carefully prepared our living room weeks in advance, nailing up an army blanket across the door to heighten our excitement. We dared not touch it, much less look in. The secret comings and goings, the transport of gifts and trains and glitter came by shadow of the night, accompanied by noise and song fortified by grog from the local pub. The crescendo built. We followed the story of Christmas each day in the local newspaper. The days dwindled down one by one. On Christmas Eve we watched the grey early evening sky for signs of Santa already on his rounds. Late at night we went back and forth on pretext to the bathroom to look across the hall until, astonishingly, the blanket would be down and all the glittering wonder of the room shone magically.

When my father died it was at Christmas time. He had prepared, as best his now weakened state could allow, a closetful of already neatly wrapped gifts. We undid each of them that morning in his absence. We undid them slowly, painfully and yet with hope, expectation and a bit of laughter at the strange preciseness, the orderliness of it all.

CIRCUS
Marc Chagall

CAFÉ TERRACE AT NIGHT

Vincent van Gogh

ON ONE HAND CELESTE, ON THE OTHER MARIE

My mistress' eyes are nothing like the sun.

WILLIAM SHAKESPEARE

The Hotel Raphael on the Rue Central was not a particularly interesting place to be a chambermaid. It was dark and musty and its usual clientele of married men in cheap brown business suits left little romantic possibility for young women. When Marie asked Celeste, then, if she would come along with her that Saturday night to the Café Miniscule, she agreed. Marie was going there to meet a man, someone recommended by her cousin.

Pascal was a musician, a drummer who played alone, occasionally accompanied by his harmonica. As they entered the narrow, crowded café, he was off in a small corner vigorously pounding his drums while sweating profusely and throwing his long, oily gray hair about his head as if in a reverie. Marie and Celeste sat at a small table and ordered glasses of red wine. As they waited for them to arrive, both noticed in the same discreet glance that Pascal, the musician, had only one arm.

"How does he manage to play?" Marie asked.

"With his feet, I guess," Celeste answered.

The one-armed drummer played on, attempting to be heard above the din of the motley cast of customers huddled in small, rowdy groups about the room. At his break, Pascal came toward their table assuming it was them he was to meet, but Marie suddenly turned cold, forcing Pascal to pass by awkwardly and sit by himself near the door. He smoked quietly, mopping his brow while sipping what Celeste thought was a small brandy. He occasionally paused to look in their direction. Celeste timidly stared back, noticing how each time he wanted to lift his glass, he methodically put down his cigarette in the ashtray.

"I'm sorry I came," Marie said, leaning over quietly.

"I suppose so," Celeste added.

Marie had barely sipped her drink when she announced that she wanted to leave. They passed him brusquely, and for most of the night Marie did not mention him again, preferring to comment on the men they watched from a distance at the next café.

The following week Celeste called Marie to say she would not be going out as usual. So on Saturday night Celeste dressed carefully before walking by herself across the Place Populare to the narrow street that ended in the Café Miniscule. She hesitated briefly at the door and seeing that Pascal was there playing his music, she went in.

A ROAD LESS TRAVELED

For the one I love most lay sleeping by me
Under the same cover in the cool night.

WALT WHITMAN

Horace was one of running's originals. Long before fitness became fashionable, he traversed the pavements of the City in isolation, wearing mainly his abbreviated underwear. Somewhat cherubic, he sported a generous brown mustache and an easy manner, though he had a voracious appetite for reading books and another unusual hobby—collecting his dreams. Horace bragged that he had volumes of notebooks filled with every detail recorded nightly as each one unpredictably appeared to him.

Horace lived with another man in an apartment in the Bronx. Though once too familiar with alcohol, he had converted to vegetarianism under Freddie's careful eye. Freddie was not a runner. He was sedentary and enjoyed waiting for Horace at the finish line, huddled in his well-worn folding chair. Thin and haggard with a rough gray beard, Freddie possessed a sharp wit and even sharper temper, especially if someone came down on the wrong side of his protégé.

One Sunday, Horace and Freddie invited our running club over for tea. We were curious and went eagerly. The apartment was threadbare: no furniture except for two folding chairs and a small coffee table. The walls were lined with books, hundreds of them. In the bathtub were two turtles, saved, they said, from imminent soup two weeks before at the Plaza Hotel. Passing hurriedly by their bedroom, I was surprised to see one large bed. The covers were rumpled as I suppose they would be on a Sunday morning. On each side of the bed was a small table with a single matching reading lamp. Two flannel nightshirts lay thrown haphazardly on the wooden floor. As I stood looking in, I realized slowly that I was seeing an intimate place where two men, men I had grown to know well in many other ways, would each night undress and sleep together.

VAN GOGH'S BEDROOM
Vincent van Gogh

TATTOO

The turtle lives 'twixt plated decks
Which practically conceal its sex.
I think it clever of the turtle
In such a fix to be so fertile.

OGDEN NASH

like a tattoo on a woman. That's not to say I like tattooed women with large fire-snorting drag-ons. No, I am talking about the small, subtle, carefully placed tattoo that is somewhat hidden and hard to find. What a delight it is when an unsuspecting bend of a shapely back or long soft-ness of an inner thigh reveals such a surprise. These subtleties are more mysterious than those placed crassly about the buttocks or the breasts or elsewhere. A tattoo is after all not meant to be a road map. If you need it for that…well.

Love has its confidences and tattoos can be just that: a small secret between you that no one else is aware of. I repeat no one. A tasteful, discreet tattoo on a woman is also enormously sensual. It wags its fetching finger at the eyes of the finder. "So now you know this about me," it says. "It is of course only a gesture at the artful inclusion of a small, rather insignificant part of myself that I have given over to this particularly interesting fantasy."

"Go on," you say. "Please don't let me interrupt. Go on."

My own views on tattoos are, however, regrettably not from experience. I have never intimate-ly known a woman with such markings and I probably won't in the future. It is not something you can ask your wife or lover to explore. No, a woman, a certain kind of woman, comes already this way. She has made this decision herself. It is part of her, a piece of her identity that follows her into her secret private life, hidden beneath an exterior patina that may even be in some cases bland and unimaginative, waiting quietly, patiently, and expecting all the while to be somehow, discovered.

LOVE SONG DURING THE NEW MOON
Paul Klee

NUDE LAKE

Bill thought it was just as well he didn't bring it up, the thing about Nude Lake and all that. After all, Lou was a customer.

"Been sometime since I've seen you, Lou."

He was staring straight into the mirror and back into Lou's beady black eyes. Bill, big-framed and big-fisted, liked to wear a short white jacket when he cut hair, buttoned up the back with a stiff round collar, like a pharmacist.

Lou said, "Just brought Bessie home, to bury her. Been living in Chicago."

"I know that," Bill said. "I heard that."

Bill was half-listening. He had gone back to that starlit night with Bessie at Nude Lake, the night after their prom. They were all celebrating. Bill had never taken off his clothes like that. Bessie and he were, let's say, not close in that way, them being the age they were at the time. He was surprised then at how easily Bessie let down her clothes and followed the rest of them down the darkened path that led to Nude Lake. Lou, of course, was there with somebody else and he disappeared eagerly in the darkness just after Bessie. Bill thought better of it, stayed behind with a few others to watch over the cars and trucks. As he sat on the running board, he could hear them frolicking in the warm, still night. Bill wasn't sure then, he still isn't sure now, about whether he'd done the right thing considering how it all turned out.

"How's that?" Bill asked.

He had just let his exquisitely honed razor graze downward along the thickly foamed side of Lou's face, finishing at the trunk of his rough-skinned neck. He stopped there and put the razor away, toweled and applied scented lotion, patting Lou's face red.

"Good. Nice, Will. It's Will, isn't it?" Lou asked.

"Close enough," Bill answered. "I suppose that's close enough."

LAKE OF FAIRIES
Martiros Sar'jan

HOLDING HANDS

And on my leaning shoulder
she laid her snow white hand.

WILLIAM BUTLER YEATS

don't see people holding hands much anymore. Too bad. It was such a comfortable, satisfying way of learning how to touch a woman. Holding hands was a first contact, a beginning, a great entrée, later of course, into a kiss. Then, too, it was a way of aimlessly strolling together, of luxuriating in each other, of mindlessly ambling, two hearts as one.

I don't know why such an easy, unimposing yet romantic gesture has gone out of vogue. I do see couples walking hand-in-hand but they seem much farther apart now, out of sync. It seems easier to hold hands, your shoulders sunk into each other, when you are younger. As adults too much is translated into it. I once tried to hold hands with a woman much taller than me who pulled me along; another, this time shorter, who dragged behind, wrenching at me like an anchor. Both were unnerving. Once, though, at the intermission of a particularly good play on Broadway as I was holding hands casually with a woman I had known for some time, she reached over as we stood quietly and placed her other hand on both of ours and shuddered excitedly as though she had been completely overcome by emotion. I was delighted to the core and have never forgotten that moment.

Then, too, it is hard to live up to the promise of such love. Yet necessarily nothing needs to be promised by holding another's hand. It is an act of friendship, of presumed closeness, of affection. It is far, far from the absolute exposure of nakedness and short by enough of two lips coming softly together. It provides you time to think, yet it gives enjoyment and warmth and the chance to look over at each other's eyes, as you meander along, to see if what you are beginning to hope is real, may at some not-too-distant point come true.

LOVERS WALKING
Giuseppe Pellizza da Volpedo

SAVOIR-FAIRE

The great days of youth when you are mispronouncing
foreign words and believing dreams.

JAMES SALTER

He and Phoebe were just friends, that's what Edgar said. On Thursday mornings they went for coffee at Jimmy's on Eighty-fifth Street to talk about how they were doing, which meant in ascending order of importance: their jobs, their friends, and where they stood when it came to love or lack thereof.

"You look glum, Edgar."

"I'm beginning to look around."

"Who for this time?"

"Someone different, someone inexperienced," he said, looking up from his cup.

"Inexperienced?" Phoebe raised her eyebrows and pushed her coffee in his direction.

Edgar took up a plastic menu and opened it, pointing down the list.

"I am with this woman at Chez Baudelaire on the Left Bank, her first night in Paris. She asks me to choose the wine, this nice Burgundy, a Nuit Saint George, this vintage—

"You are pointing to the Reuben sandwich, Edgar."

He ignored her and continued on.

"Her eyes are lighting up as we touch glasses, the soft spring breeze ruffling ever so slightly the locks of her light-brown hair-"

"Oo-la-la, Edgar. Quel panache!" Phoebe interrupted.

He smiled. "I like that word."

"Sounds like a dance, doesn't it?" she said.

"Taking lessons."

"You are? How suave, Edgar."

He shrugged sheepishly.

"You know"—Phoebe leaned forward more earnestly—"It's not necessary to try so hard to impress, Edgar. At least not in your case."

"Well…" he hesitated.

"Keep it simple."

"I'd love to do that," he said.

Phoebe stared back more intently now into Edgar's unguarded blue eyes.

"Me too," she added.

PARIS: AUTEIL

Maurice Utrillo

LA CHAHUT
Georges Seurat

THE VERY LAST NUPTIAL
OF NICK SARDI

And hand in hand, on the edge of the sand,
They danced by the light of the moon.

EDWARD LEAR

My grandfather, Nick Sardi, sat me down one night before he died and told me about his three weddings. He was young the first time. When his father-in-law, unrenowned for his generosity, offered five hundred dollars for the whole affair adding "If I were you I'd take it and put it in my pocket," Nick took this as a challenge. On the morning of the ceremony, he was frantically mopping down a musty Goodfellows Hall before propping up a 75-pound fan high above the dance floor to cool the engines of the prospective revelers. There were many, who drank profusely and shook the rafters, causing the fan at times to teeter precariously above the din. The guests were eclectic and included a Japanese woman dressed in traditional attire. When his cousin, Lou Vecchione, stumbled over to her and said he remembered her from Kobe, my grandfather ran for him but not before Lou passed out at the feet of the woman's husband who my grandfather said was very gracious.

The second knot-tying fifteen years later was less spontaneous, even a bit staged. It was the old story of picturing a happy scene and then trying to make it happen. Nick picked a rural church in the countryside near Amenia, a place he was particularly fond of. The February day met him with brilliant sunshine and glimmering snow-covered cornfields. He led the wedding party through the hills and valleys in his 1948 Cadillac to a log cabin inn perched on a frozen lake near Oregon Corners. The merriment was more forced, he thought, the mood of the guests reticent. Nick took this as an omen. After that, my grandfather took a rest, a long rest. When I asked what that meant, he answered quickly, "figuratively of course." The repose lasted better than ten years. Until the final wedding.

"I once pictured myself being married in an ornate palazzo along the Grand Canal in Venice," he said, "late at night, everyone arriving by coach announced by the clicking of the hooves on the wet cobblestone."

The next New Year's Eve, Nick found himself in the center hall of a mansion overlooking the Hudson River. His beautiful young bride walked down a flowing staircase to the marble floor of the atrium. The men were all in black tie, the women stylish, some with extravagant hats. Just before twelve, the justice, who wore a patch over one eye, gracefully presided. Nick's daughters read poems and scripture. There were toasts and dancing, a genuine good time. Nick was relaxed and, this time, didn't keep one eye on the ceiling fan above. When New Year's Day had well begun, the party drifted into a vast side room dominated by a huge glowing fireplace. His long time friends spoke masterfully in tribute of the occasion before his neighbor, Eddie Nicoletti, a well-known club singer, sang "La Vie En Rose." Nick and his bride were enraptured.

My grandfather can't sing, at least I never heard him. When the song was over, a lull came over the room. Someone said, "Get up there Nick and say something. Do something." He hesitated. Nothing came to mind. What could sum up the experience of that night, highlight the happiness he felt at being there. He slowly began humming a Puccini aria that his father used to sing to him. The words began to flow as the sweat dripped off his forehead and his hands trembled at his side. "O mio bambino caro." On he went in spirited half-broken notes, his voice gathering ground until his arms were waving and his chin rose proudly high. His face was red with excitement and he finished with a joyous flourish standing there beaming at the wildly applauding guests.

"What happened after that?" I asked.

My grandfather reached into his pocket for his handkerchief and mopped his brow.

"That's about it," he said, "it came out pretty good in the end," he hesitated and then smiled.

DAUGHTERS

My thoughts are children
With uneasy faces
That awake and rise
Beneath running skies.

PHILIP LARKIN

We were going north that Christmas evening to Lake Placid, my two daughters and I, by train. I had spent the first year of my life there near White Face Mountain. As other families settled into the warmth of their holiday living rooms, we retraced my journey watching the ice-covered Hudson River speed by in the slate white sunset.

The trip was our chance to be together, to be away from some of Christmas's customs now become uncomfortable. We were, the three of us, refugees from the season of divorce, a season whose sad vapors drifted most pervasively into this time of the year.

The train's cabin seemed at first foreign and we remained quiet with one another, reading, silently apart. But as the black, light-dotted silhouettes of Albany passed, we had already begun to chat more, to laugh and play cards and backgammon, to enjoy the brightness and comfort of our now lived-in seats. Slowly our eyes grew heavy as the train raced excitedly in the night, rolling side to side, slowing to blow methodically its sonorous horn as we passed through snow fields obscure and silent save for a lone farmhouse light bulb peeking out of the darkness.

My children slept and I watched silently, so happy and content to be with them. Three renegades on the rails were we, lurching, galloping ahead on steel wings into the promising vastness until we reached Westport at the end of Lake Champlain, our stop. The yellow-lit station was covered in fresh snow, undisturbed on such a holiday. We dragged our baggage across to where a solitary taxi was waiting, its exhaust puffing crystals in the bitter night air. Placing our bags in the trunk, we pushed cozily into the backseat.

"Take us to Lake Placid," we said unhesitatingly in one voice.

"Back home," I added softly.

GIRLS ON THE EDGE OF WATER
Pierre-Auguste Renoir

WHEN SILENCE
IS AN ANSWER

Music when soft voices die
Vibrates in the memory.

PERCY BYSSHE SHELLEY

When I was young and needed to talk more about myself and how I felt about the unsteady world before me, I found the friendship I sought around the crackling flames of a campfire. My friends and I, shrouded securely by the blackness of the night, would sit quietly addressing the glowing embers, never really speaking directly to one another, but relying on everyone to understand and respond in the oblique, measured manner of adolescent boys. Those nights lifted us from isolation and for a while made us united with one another rendering us later, much later, the better for it.

In college, the discourse changed ever so slightly. We still felt the need to be together in the sports we played, to linger idly in the dormitory rooms, crowded together on unmade beds or perched on chairs turned backwards to listen carefully to a weekend caper or more so, to the discontents we felt as students before the inequities of the world as we were learning it.

Now as an adult close friendships seem more difficult to nurture and sustain, yet it is strangely simpler to feel the comfort of one's friends. Though competition in all its forms has driven us apart; for success, for money, for women, for power and esteem—there is in friendship now a greater clarity, our strengths and foibles more easily accepted. Those subtle moments seem now to mean the most: a compliment unexpected, a visit in a time of illness, reciting Yeats together in front of a fire over whiskey, a comforting pat on the back in difficulty, time unmeasured when time alone can cure, a sure opinion when silence is an answer, the risk of criticizing or giving advice even in the affairs of love, true pleasure at one another's success, and, perhaps most of all, the profound mutual joy of just knowing and having known one another.

THE ROCKS IN THE PARK OF THE CHATEAU NOIR
Paul Cezanne

LETTING GO

Running water never disappointed.
Crossing water always furthered something.
Stepping stones are stations of the soul.

SEAMUS HEANEY

"Get back into the car."

I did, but I couldn't help looking behind me once more.

"Let's go," my mother said, "you will only make it worse."

My daughter, my oldest child, had turned and begun walking up the path into the woods. She was carrying a fresh new duffel bag on her shoulder. She was only eleven. It was her first time going away from home, to a camp in Pennsylvania. We had just driven over eight hours to get there.

I turned the key and silently, instinctively brought the car around, then coasted down the rutted dirt road until it turned into macadam, hesitated, and put my foot down firmly on the gas pedal.

"I think she'll be okay," I said sadly at the now quick-moving highway ahead.

When my second daughter went to riding camp in Vermont a year later, I thought it would be easier, but it wasn't. As I was about to leave, tears welled up in her eyes yet she quickly helped me by saying she'd better join the girls already fixing their bunks. She turned one last time toward me as she walked purposefully back and entered her silent nervous dormitory.

Both of these moments marked a change in our lives. For my daughters, it was a chance to begin moving into spheres outside their homes, to measure themselves, to compare their lives to date with others their age. For me, it was accepting that their maturity had now begun. They would grow more emotionally, would be challenged and, for the first time, they would be truly alone. This change came hard for me. I acutely felt the separation. It penetrated deep into my very insides as a queasy unhappiness that would take sometime to leave. Yet it was the right thing, to give them these chances. I wanted then, as I do now, everything that can be considered good for my daughters. Yet, loving one's children so much is knowing and accepting, even if reluctantly, when the time has come to let go.

LE DUNE
Ettore Tito

REDHEAD

I had a sense of coming home to myself, and of having found out
What a little circle man's experience is.

WILLA CATHER

My wife has long hair that seems to get into everything— the scrambled eggs, my toothbrush, and even our baby's diaper. I really don't mind it. There was a time when I would have but now I kind of like the idea of her being around. The strands of hair are a pleasant reminder, a way of discovering her in different places.

It was not that long ago that I wanted my front car seats clean with no trace of anyone. I liked the orderly, antiseptic sense of it. But that has slowly changed. Those long curly threads of deep red hair are now welcome and when they turn up as I drive, my thoughts turn to her. I even sometimes weaken to envy, knowing her hair is so rich and beautiful that she can afford to unknowingly lose some. Unlike me.

Living again with someone takes time, more than I thought it would, though putting your soiled socks everyday in the same washing machine has a strange way of bringing you closer together. I wish there were a formula for a successful relationship but there is not. My best general advice is to think a bit longer about whatever conflict is brewing and then hold your tongue. I don't always follow such advice but, on a totally unrelated note, I do enjoy finding the unexpected strand of my wife's hair, preferably not in the bathroom sink or in the kitchen. Better, I like them mixed up mischievously in my clothes, long stubborn curls of red hair pulled from my shorts and socks and tee shirts. Often I just leave them there. They're comfortable and familiar and have come to feel so good close to my skin.